Guest Book to Celebrate

____

____

Event Date

____

THANK YOU FOR COMING.

Let's celebrate!

SPACE FOR
A PHOTO

Guest Name

Thoughts & Messages

Email/Phone

Guest Name

Thoughts & Messages

Email/Phone

Guest Name

Thoughts & Messages

Email/Phone

Guest Name

Thoughts & Messages

EMAIL/PHONE

Guest Name

Thoughts & Messages

Email/Phone

Guest Name

Thoughts & Messages

Email/Phone

Guest Name

Thoughts & Messages

Email/Phone

Guest Name

Thoughts & Messages

EMAIL/PHONE

Guest Name

Thoughts & Messages

Email/Phone

Guest Name

Thoughts & Messages

Email/Phone

Guest Name

Thoughts & Messages

Email/Phone

Guest Name

Thoughts & Messages

Email/Phone

Guest Name

Thoughts & Messages

Email/Phone

Guest Name

Thoughts & Messages

Email/Phone

Guest Name

Thoughts & Messages

Email/Phone

Guest Name

Thoughts & Messages

Email/Phone

Guest Name

Thoughts & Messages

Email/Phone

Guest Name

Thoughts & Messages

Email/Phone

Guest Name

Thoughts & Messages

EMAIL/PHONE

Guest Name

Thoughts & Messages

Email/Phone

Guest Name

Thoughts & Messages

Email/Phone

Guest Name

Thoughts & Messages

Email/Phone

Guest Name

Thoughts & Messages

Email/Phone

Guest Name

Thoughts & Messages

Email/Phone

Guest Name

Thoughts & Messages

Email/Phone

Guest Name

Thoughts & Messages

Email/Phone

Guest Name

Thoughts & Messages

Email/Phone

Guest Name

Thoughts & Messages

Email/Phone

Guest Name

Thoughts & Messages

Email/Phone

Guest Name

Thoughts & Messages

Email/Phone

Guest Name

Thoughts & Messages

Email/Phone

Guest Name

Thoughts & Messages

Email/Phone

Guest Name

Thoughts & Messages

Email/Phone

Guest Name

Thoughts & Messages

Email/Phone

Guest Name

Thoughts & Messages

Email/Phone

Guest Name

Thoughts & Messages

Email/Phone

Guest Name

Thoughts & Messages

Email/Phone

Guest Name

Thoughts & Messages

Email/Phone

Guest Name

Thoughts & Messages

Email/Phone

Guest Name

Thoughts & Messages

Email/Phone

Guest Name

Thoughts & Messages

Email/Phone

Guest Name

Thoughts & Messages

Email/Phone

Guest Name

Thoughts & Messages

Email/Phone

Guest Name

Thoughts & Messages

Email/Phone

Guest Name

Thoughts & Messages

Email/Phone

Guest Name

Thoughts & Messages

Email/Phone

Guest Name

Thoughts & Messages

Email/Phone

Guest Name

Thoughts & Messages

Email/Phone

Guest Name

Thoughts & Messages

Email/Phone

Guest Name

Thoughts & Messages

Email/Phone

Guest Name

Thoughts & Messages

Email/Phone

Guest Name

Thoughts & Messages

Email/Phone

Guest Name

Thoughts & Messages

Email/Phone

Guest Name

Thoughts & Messages

Email/Phone

Guest Name

Thoughts & Messages

Email/Phone

Guest Name

Thoughts & Messages

Email/Phone

Guest Name

Thoughts & Messages

Email/Phone

Guest Name

Thoughts & Messages

Email/Phone

Guest Name

Thoughts & Messages

Email/Phone

Guest Name

Thoughts & Messages

Email/Phone

Guest Name

Thoughts & Messages

Email/Phone

Guest Name

Thoughts & Messages

Email/Phone

Guest Name

Thoughts & Messages

Email/Phone

Guest Name

Thoughts & Messages

EMAIL/PHONE

Guest Name

Thoughts & Messages

Email/Phone

Guest Name

Thoughts & Messages

Email/Phone

Guest Name

Thoughts & Messages

Email/Phone

Guest Name

Thoughts & Messages

Email/Phone

Guest Name

Thoughts & Messages

Email/Phone

Guest Name

Thoughts & Messages

EMAIL/PHONE

Guest Name

Thoughts & Messages

Email/Phone

Guest Name

Thoughts & Messages

E

EMAIL/PHONE

Guest Name

Thoughts & Messages

Email/Phone

Guest Name

Thoughts & Messages

Email/Phone

Guest Name

Thoughts & Messages

Email/Phone

Guest Name

Thoughts & Messages

Email/Phone

Guest Name

Thoughts & Messages

Email/Phone

Guest Name

Thoughts & Messages

Email/Phone

Guest Name

Thoughts & Messages

Email/Phone

Guest Name

Thoughts & Messages

Email/Phone

Guest Name

Thoughts & Messages

Email/Phone

Guest Name

Thoughts & Messages

Email/Phone

Guest Name

Thoughts & Messages

Email/Phone

Guest Name

Thoughts & Messages

EMAIL/PHONE

Guest Name

Thoughts & Messages

Email/Phone

Guest Name

Thoughts & Messages

Email/Phone

Guest Name

Thoughts & Messages

Email/Phone

Guest Name

Thoughts & Messages

Email/Phone

Guest Name

Thoughts & Messages

Email/Phone

Guest Name

Thoughts & Messages

Email/Phone

Guest Name

Thoughts & Messages

Email/Phone

Guest Name

Thoughts & Messages

Email/Phone

Guest Name

Thoughts & Messages

Email/Phone

Guest Name

Thoughts & Messages

Email/Phone

Guest Name

Thoughts & Messages

EMAIL/PHONE

Guest Name

Thoughts & Messages

Email/Phone

Guest Name

Thoughts & Messages

Email/Phone

Guest Name

Thoughts & Messages

Email/Phone

Guest Name

Thoughts & Messages

Email/Phone

Guest Name

Thoughts & Messages

Email/Phone

Guest Name

Thoughts & Messages

Email/Phone

Guest Name

Thoughts & Messages

Email/Phone

Guest Name

Thoughts & Messages

Email/Phone

Guest Name

Thoughts & Messages

EMAIL/PHONE

Guest Name

Thoughts & Messages

Email/Phone

Guest Name

Thoughts & Messages

Email/Phone

Guest Name

Thoughts & Messages

Email/Phone

Guest Name

Thoughts & Messages

Email/Phone

Guest Name

Thoughts & Messages

Email/Phone

Guest Name

Thoughts & Messages

Email/Phone

GIFT LOG

Name /Email /Phone	Gift

GIFT LOG

Name /Email /Phone	Gift

GIFT LOG

Name /Email /Phone	Gift

GIFT LOG

Name /Email /Phone	Gift

GIFT LOG

Name /Email /Phone	Gift

GIFT LOG

Name /Email /Phone	Gift

GIFT LOG

Name /Email /Phone	Gift

GIFT LOG

Name /Email /Phone	Gift

GIFT LOG

Name /Email /Phone	Gift

GIFT LOG

Name /Email /Phone	Gift

Made in United States
Orlando, FL
09 July 2023